Abounding
Faith

A TREASURY OF WISDOM

EDITED, WITH COMMENTARY, BY

M. Scott Peck, M.D.

AUTHOR OF THE ROAD LESS TRAVELED

ACKNOWLEDGMENT

Since a number of quotes in this anthology were gathered from
Lessons at the Halfway Point: Wisdom for Midlife by Michael Levine,
I would specifically like to thank my friend, Michael, for donating
them to this work. They are, however, copyrighted by him, and are
not for general use without his permission.

03   04   05   06   07   KWF   10   9   8   7   6   5   4   3   2   1

ISBN: 0-7407-3334-6
Library of Congress Catalog Card Number: 2002111563

contents

preface

In 2000, M. Scott Peck edited a collection of his favorite quotations in a beautiful volume called *Abounding Grace: An Anthology of Wisdom*. These words, gleaned from writers and thinkers, both famous and obscure, ancient and modern, were chosen to serve as guideposts on the road to a more spiritual existence.

Abounding Faith is developed from one of the twelve sections of *Abounding Grace*. The book not only includes all the quotations from the Faith section of *Abounding Grace* and Dr. Peck's introductory commentary, but a number of new quotations as well.

introduction

*M*Y PRIMARY IDENTITY, before that of a religious person, is that of a scientist. We scientists are empiricists, meaning believers in empiricism. Empiricism is the philosophy that the best—not the only, but the best—route to knowledge is through experience. That is why we conduct experiments—controlled experiences to gain knowledge.

In this respect I am very much like Carl Jung. Toward the end of his long life the media decided to do a film interview with him to capture him for posterity. To me it was a rather inane interview until its conclusion, when the reporter asked, "Professor

Jung, a lot of your writings have a religious flavor. Do you believe in God?"

"Believe in God?" old Jung repeated, as best as I can recall, puffing on his pipe thoughtfully. "Well, believe is a word we use when we think that something is true, but for which we do not yet have a substantial body of evidence. No. No, I don't believe in God. I *know* there's a God."

I have faith in God because I have seen the evidence. But, you might ask, is faith earned or is it a gift, perhaps even more of a gift than any of the other virtues? Later in this book, we will read these words from St. Paul: "By grace are ye saved through faith; and that not of yourselves: it is the gift of God." As far as I am concerned, no truer words were ever spoken. I would simply elaborate that in my personal case it has been God who reached down to me through His grace to open my eyes so that I might see the evidence of His footprints at almost every turn.

Make no mistake; it is a gift. The fact is that many—if not most—people never see the evidence. But how can they not see it? Or hear it? How can they not hear the "still, small voice" of God within them, speaking with a wisdom beyond the capacity of their own brains?

I am reminded of a rather critical review of my early work. The review ended by concluding something to the effect: "These books are not particularly consoling to those of us who do not, like Peck, seem to have a direct phone line to God."

I wrote a note back to the reviewer to suggest that her conclusion might be slightly misleading. "If I have a direct phone line to God," I informed her, "frankly, most of the time the machine doesn't work. But yes, upon occasion it does ring." What I didn't add, out of possibly misplaced kindness, was the fact that many people permanently leave their phone off the hook.

But why? Why would they leave it off the hook? It is an excellent question to which the answers are multiple, complex, and still ultimately mysterious. For the sake of brevity let me simply once more quote St. Paul: "It is a terrifying thing to fall into the hands of the living God." There is a certain loss of control involved that many people either will not or cannot bear.

The ability or willingness to bear it is itself a gift. Yes, faith is indeed a gift. This doesn't mean the gift cannot be sought after and nurtured, however; it most definitely can be. The seeking and nurturance of faith is what I would call "healthy piety."

Piety can be simply defined as "the practice of religious faith." The chapter that follows on this subject is remarkably brief. This is because *public* piety is so frequently not a virtue. Indeed, it is often a vice, an unhealthy practice of self-satisfaction and self-aggrandizement that may actually interfere with faith development. It is no accident that Jesus railed against it. Yet healthy piety is a terribly important matter. Let me redress the poverty of quotes herein by focusing the remainder of this introduction on it, bearing in mind that I shall be talking of piety that is *private,* sometimes even deliberately hidden.

One stumbling block to the silent seeking for God that is healthy piety is the sense of many rational people that they must have God all figured out before they can have faith in Him (or Her). This is under-standable but excessively self-reliant. Because God is so much bigger than we are, we can never get Him pinned to the wall like a butterfly we can study at our leisure. You will never completely understand God the way God can understand you. Complete understanding of God as a precondition for faith is an impossible illusion. This is why St. Augustine proclaimed: "Do not seek to understand that you might have faith; seek faith that you might understand." It is a glorious message. Not only does it make the sequence correct, but it rightly implies that the acquisition of faith will open our eyes to a whole new level of understanding.

By agreeing completely with St. Augustine that a healthy faith in God precedes a deep understanding of this world, in no way do I mean to discourage healthy doubt or questioning. In the quotes to follow I deliberately included several that extol doubting. By doubt I don't mean atheism—the certainty that God does not exist. I mean agnosticism—the not-knowing, the questioning of God's ways and even the questioning of His very existence. Such questioning is usually a necessary step in the movement from a simplistic, hand-me-down faith to a faith of mature simplicity that lies "on the other side of complexity." Indeed, I believe that this kind of doubt should be, in itself, considered one of the great religious virtues. Use your mind. Think for yourself, for God's sake!

But do it well. If you are going to get good at this business of doubting, then you are ultimately going to need to learn how to doubt your own doubts. Three decades ago I ran into a strange little gnome of an old man, living in the woods, who had been gifted with a genius for composing couplets of wisdom. One of them was: "If you want to know what God is all about / then why not try giving Him the benefit of the doubt?"

As in this matter of faith preceding understanding, there is another way that my notion of piety was turned topsy-turvy. About a decade ago I happened to run across an ancient Christian proverb, so ancient it was in Latin, reading *"Lex orandi, lex credendi."* Literally translated it says, "The rule of prayer precedes the rule of belief." Until that moment I'd imagined that if I had a lot of faith, then I would pray a lot. But now this proverb was telling me the opposite: that if I prayed a lot, then—and perhaps only then—I would grow in faith. The proverb has the sequence right.

The subject of prayer, or remembering God, is as complex as modern medicine. There are dozens of different ways of praying, and it would be unfitting for me to delve deeply into the complexity here. Suffice it to say that one of the many ways the matter can be categorized is to divide it into public prayer and private prayer. Although public prayer is not without its virtue, herein I am referring to private prayer: the kind of prayer you do alone in your study or bedroom, including prayers of doubt. It is this kind of prayer, usually silent and hidden, that I am preaching as the primary path for seeking the gift of faith or "spiritual growth."

Fifteen years ago I was involved with a team of people that included a young woman I'll call Mary. Mary was then a vocally "fundamentalist" Christian. She seemed unable to speak more than two sentences in sequence without at least one of them including the reverentially intoned name of Jesus. This caused considerable friction. Because I was at the time something of a mentor to her, Mary came to me to ask why she was seemingly alienating the other members of the team.

"It's because of your piety," I explained. "You're so public about it, they feel they're being preached to, and they resent it. They want you as a teammate, not a preacher."

"But what can I do about it?" she inquired in total innocence.

"What you shouldn't do about it is give up a shred of your faith," I responded. "What you should do is to keep it private. You know," I continued, "I've heard tell of certain Christian monks and nuns who upon occasion practice a strange kind of spiritual discipline. They take a vow—just as they would a vow of poverty or chastity or obedience—to not speak the name of Jesus out loud for a year. They remain free to use his name in their hearts and private prayer, but they renounce their need to speak it publicly. As I said, it's a strange kind of discipline, but I wonder if it wouldn't be a useful one for you at this particular point."

I am unaccustomed to my advice being followed to the letter. But to my amazement, over the year that followed Mary never mentioned Jesus at any team meeting. She rapidly became one of the most successful and constructive team members. After the year she confessed to me she'd not only kept her vow on the team but with all the other friends in her life. "It's bizarre," she said. "Jesus has become ever more important to me over the past year, but I no longer have the slightest need to talk about him."

This has been a mere vignette. But let me say this: I have never seen anyone grow so rapidly, not only in that year but in the years to follow. Indeed, it was not long before Mary had become *my* mentor and one of the greatest spiritual leaders it has been my privilege to know.

enthusiasm

*I*t seems to me we can never give up longing and wishing while we are thoroughly alive. There are certain things we feel to be beautiful and good, and we must hunger after them.

—George Eliot

A certain excessiveness seems a necessary element in all greatness.

—Harvey Cushing

*I*n things pertaining to enthusiasm, no man is
sane who does not know how to be insane
on proper occasions.
— HENRY WARD BEECHER

I prefer the folly of enthusiasm to the
indifference of wisdom.
— ANATOLE FRANCE

*Y*ou need to get up in the morning and say, "Boy,
I'm going to—in my own stupid way—save
the world today."
— SALLY BERGER

The world belongs to the enthusiast who
keeps cool.
—WILLIAM McFEE

You can't sweep other people off their feet if you
can't be swept off your own.
—CLARENCE DAY

You must learn day by day, year by year, to
broaden your horizon. The more things you
love, the more you are interested in, the more
you enjoy, the more you are indignant about,
the more you have left when anything happens.
—ETHEL BARRYMORE

*Z*est is the secret of all beauty. There is no beauty that is attractive without zest.
———CHRISTIAN DIOR

*L*et us live while we live.
———PHILIP DOORIDGE

*T*he trouble with some women is that they get all excited about nothing—and then marry him.
———CHER

*N*othing is interesting if you're not interested.
———HELEN MACINNES

The sense of this word among the Greeks affords the noblest definition of it; enthusiasm signifies "God in us."
—MADAME DE STAEL

Indifference may not wreck a man's life at any one turn, but it will destroy him with a kind of dry-rot in the long run.
—BLISS CARMAN

A man can be short and dumpy and getting bald but if he has fire, women will like him.
—MAE WEST

Every production of genius must be the production
of enthusiasm.
———BENJAMIN DISRAELI

Life is a romantic business. It is painting a
picture, not doing a sum—but you have to
make the romance, and it will come to the
question how much fire you have in your belly.
———OLIVER WENDELL HOLMES JR.

Alas! How enthusiasm decreases, as our
experience increases!
———LOUISE COLET

*I*ndifference never wrote great works, nor thought out striking inventions, nor reared the solemn architecture that awes the soul, nor breathed sublime music, nor painted glorious pictures, nor undertook heroic philanthropies. All these grandeurs are born of enthusiasm, and are done heartily.

—ANONYMOUS

*G*od writes my music.

—JOHANN SEBASTIAN BACH

*L*ack of pep is often mistaken for patience.

—KIN HUBBARD

*I*f you aren't fired with enthusiasm, you will be fired with enthusiasm.
———Vince Lombardi

I am not eccentric. It's just that I am more alive than most people. I am an unpopular electric eel set in a pond of goldfish.
———Dame Edith Sitwell

*I*f a man is called to be a street sweeper, he should sweep streets even as Michelangelo painted or Beethoven composed music or Shakespeare wrote poetry.
———Martin Luther King Jr.

*W*hen a man dies, if he can pass enthusiasm
along to his children, he has left them an estate
of incalculable value.

—THOMAS ALVA EDISON

*T*here is nothing so easy but it becomes difficult
when you do it reluctantly.

—TERENCE

*D*on't ever let me catch you singing like that
again, without enthusiasm. You're nothing if
you aren't excited by what you're doing.

—FRANK SINATRA TO HIS SON,
FRANK JR.

*K*nowledge is power, but enthusiasm pulls the switch.

—IVERN BELL

*E*ven virtue itself, all perfect as it is, requires to be inspirited by passion; for duties are but coldly performed which are but philosophically fulfilled.

—ANNA JAMESON

*O*ne can never consent to creep when one feels an impulse to soar.

—HELEN KELLER

*E*nthusiasm is a divine possession.
— MARGARET E. SANGSTER

*I*t is the greatest shot of adrenaline to be doing
what you've wanted to do so badly. You almost
feel like you could fly without the plane.
— CHARLES LINDBERGH

*I*t takes great passion and great energy to do anything creative, especially in the theater. You
have to care so much that you can't sleep, you
can't eat, you can't talk to people. It's just got to
be right. You can't do it without that passion.
— AGNES DeMILLE

*E*very day's a kick!

—OPRAH WINFREY

*E*nthusiasm is contagious. Be a carrier.

—SUSAN RABIN AND
BARBARA LAGOWSKI

*E*xuberance is Beauty.

—WILLIAM BLAKE

*A*lways give them the old fire, even when you
feel like a squashed cake of ice.

—ETHEL MERMAN

*J*ump into the middle of things, get your hands
dirty, fall flat on your face, and then reach for
the stars.
—JOAN L. CURCIO

*W*hatever you attempt, go at it with spirit.
Put some in!
—DAVID STARR JORDAN

*T*here is real magic in enthusiasm. It spells
the difference between mediocrity and
accomplishment.
—NORMAN VINCENT PEALE

*I*t is for us to pray not for tasks equal to our powers, but for powers equal to our tasks, to go forward with a great desire forever beating at the door of our hearts as we travel towards our distant goal.

—HELEN KELLER

*B*e fanatics. When it comes to being and going and dreaming of the best, *be maniacs.*

—A. M. ROSENTHAL

*L*et a man in a garret but burn with enough intensity and he will set fire to the world.

—ANTOINE DE SAINT-EXUPÉRY

grace

By grace are ye saved through faith; and that
not of yourselves: it is the gift of God.

—EPHESIANS 2:8

Amazing grace! How sweet the sound,
That saved a wretch like me;
I once was lost, but now I'm found;
Was blind, but now I see.

—JOHN NEWTON

*G*race fills empty spaces, but it can only enter where there is a void to receive it, and it is grace itself which makes this void.

—SIMONE WEIL

*G*race is but glory begun, and glory is but grace perfected.

—JONATHAN EDWARDS

*G*race is not a strange, magic substance which is subtly filtered into our souls to act as a kind of spiritual penicillin. Grace is unity, oneness within ourselves, oneness with God.

—THOMAS MERTON

The religious who, of course, ascribe the origins of grace to God, believing it to be literally God's love, have through the ages had the same difficulty locating God. There are within theology two lengthy and opposing traditions in this regard: one, the doctrine of Emanance, which holds that grace emanates down from an external God to men; the other the doctrine of Immanence, which holds that grace emanates out from the God within the center of man's being.

—M. SCOTT PECK

What is grace? I know until you ask me; when you ask me, I do not know.

—SAINT AUGUSTINE

All men who live with any degree of serenity live by some assurance of grace.

—REINHOLD NIEBUHR

I would like to achieve a state of inner spiritual grace from which I could function and give as I was meant to in the eye of God.

—ANNE MORROW LINDBERGH

*T*he grace of God is in my mind shaped like a key,
that comes from time to time and unlocks the
heavy doors.

—DONALD SWAN

*G*ive us grace and strength to forbear and to
persevere. Give us courage and gaiety and the
quiet mind, spare to us our friends, soften to
us our enemies.

—ROBERT LOUIS STEVENSON

*G*race strikes us when we are in great pain and restlessness. . . . Sometimes at that moment a wave of light breaks into our darkness, and it is as though a voice were saying: "You are accepted."

—PAUL JOHANNES TILLICH

*G*race is nothing else but a certain beginning of glory in us.

—SAINT THOMAS AQUINAS

*A*ll is waiting and all is work; all is change and all is permanence. All is grace.

—BARBARA GRIZZUTI HARRISON

*I*t is not in virtue of its liberty that the human will
attains to grace, it is much rather by grace that
it attains to liberty.
—SAINT AUGUSTINE

*G*race was in all her steps,
Heaven in her eye.
In Every gesture dignity and love.
—JOHN MILTON

*R*eligion in its humility restores man to his only
dignity, the courage to live by grace.
—GEORGE SANTAYANA

God does not refuse grace to one who does what he can.

—MEDIEVAL LATIN PROVERB

Grace is not something that comes in from the outside and says, "No, you are doing it wrong, let me show you how to do it." Grace is not a kind of auxiliary steam, supplementing our feeble powers with a force not of the same character. Grace does not replace nature, it perfects nature, transmutes something that belongs to earth and makes it glow with the radiance of heaven.

—RONALD A. KNOX

Hope

While I breathe, I hope.

—Medieval proverb

"Hope" is the thing with feathers
That perches in the soul—
And sings the tune without
And never stops—at all.

—Emily Dickinson

*W*e must accept finite disappointment, but we must never lose infinite hope.
—MARTIN LUTHER KING JR.

*H*ope is independent of the apparatus of logic.
—NORMAN COUSINS

*H*ope is the pillar that holds up the world. Hope is the dream of a waking man.
—PLINY THE ELDER

A good hope is better than a poor possession.
—SPANISH PROVERB

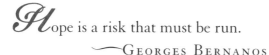

*H*ope is a risk that must be run.

—GEORGES BERNANOS

*H*ope is a prodigal young heir, and Experience is
his banker.

—CHARLES CALEB COLTON

*W*hen hope is taken away from a people moral
degeneration follows swiftly after.

—PEARL S. BUCK

*H*ope for the best, but prepare for the worst.

—ENGLISH PROVERB

*H*ope is the source of all happiness. . . . None is to be considered a man who does not hope in God.
———Philo

*B*lessed is the man that trusteth in the Lord, and whose hope the Lord is.
———Jeremiah 17: 7

*I*n the time of trouble avert not thy face from hope, for the soft marrow abideth in the hard bone.
———Hafiz

*H*ope is the best possession. None are completely wretched but those who are without hope, and few are reduced so low as that.

— WILLIAM HAZLITT

*B*efore you focus on finding the right person, concentrate on being the right person.

— MICHAEL LEVINE

*H*ope is necessary in every condition. The miseries of poverty, sickness, of captivity, would, without this comfort, be insupportable.

— SAMUEL JOHNSON

*A*ppetite, with an opinion of attaining, is called
hope; the same, without such opinion, despair.
—THOMAS HOBBES

*W*e should not let our fears hold us back from
pursuing our hopes.
—JOHN F. KENNEDY

*H*ope has as many lives as a cat or a king.
—HENRY WADSWORTH LONGFELLOW

*H*ope is the poor man's bread.
—GEORGE HERBERT

*N*ever give out while there is hope; but hope not
    beyond reason, for that shows more desire than
    judgment.
                    —WILLIAM PENN

*G*reat hopes make great men.
                    —THOMAS FULLER, M.D.

*I*n the land of hope there is never any Winter.
                    —RUSSIAN PROVERB

*I*f hoping does you any good, hope on.
                    —C. M. WIELAND

*H*ope is the feeling you have that the feeling you have isn't permanent.

—JEAN KERR

*T*here is hope for all of us. Well, anyway, if you don't die you live through it, day in, day out.

—MARY BECKETT

*T*o eat bread without hope is still slowly to starve to death.

—PEARL S. BUCK

We all hope for a—must I say the word—recipe, we all believe, however much we know we shouldn't, that maybe somebody's got that recipe and can show us how not to be sick, suffer, and die.
———NAN SHIN

Hope is a very unruly emotion.
———GLORIA STEINEM

The natural flights of the human mind are not from pleasure to pleasure, but from hope to hope.
———SAMUEL JOHNSON

They say Despair has power to kill
With her bleak frown; but I say No;
If life did hang upon her will,
Then Hope had perish'd long ago;
Yet still the twain keep up their "barful strife."
—HARTLEY COLERIDGE

Something will turn up.
—BENJAMIN DISRAELI

There is no medicine like hope, no incentive so
great, and no tonic so powerful as expectation
of something better tomorrow.
—ORISON MARDEN

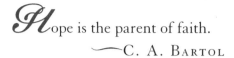

*H*ope is the parent of faith.

——C. A. BARTOL

*M*ore pleasure in hope than in fulfillment.

——JAPANESE PROVERB

*E*verything that is done in the world is done by hope.

——MARTIN LUTHER

*T*he hope, and not the fact, of advancement is the spur to industry.

——HENRY TAYLOR

Hope is a strange invention—
A Patent of the Heart—
In unremitting action
Yet never wearing out—.
———EMILY DICKINSON

Take from a man his wealth, and you hinder him;
take from him his purpose, and you slow him
down. But take from man his hope, and you
stop him. He can go on without wealth, and
even without purpose, for awhile. But he will
not go on without hope.
———C. NEIL STRAIT

Cathedrals are an unassailable witness to human passion. Using what demented calculation could an animal build such places? I think we know. An animal with a gorgeous genius for hope.

—LIONEL TIGER

The human body experiences a powerful gravitational pull in the direction of hope. That is why the patient's hopes are the physician's secret weapon. They are the hidden ingredients in any prescription.

—NORMAN COUSINS

Some one once said to me, "Reverend Schuller,
I hope you live to see all your dreams fulfilled."
I replied, "I hope not, because if I live and
all my dreams are fulfilled, I'm dead." It's
unfulfilled dreams that keep you alive.
—ROBERT SCHULLER

What oxygen is to the lungs, such is hope to the
meaning of life.
—EMIL BRUNNER

In Israel, in order to be a realist, you must believe
in miracles.
—DAVID BEN-GURION

If one truly has lost hope, one would not be on
  hand to say so.
  —Eric Bentley

He that wants hope is the poorest man alive.
  —Thomas Fuller, M.D.

If a man like Malcolm X could change and
  repudiate racism, if I myself and other former
  Muslims can change, if young whites can
  change, then there is hope for America.
  —Eldridge Cleaver

To travel hopefully is better than to arrive.
—SIR JAMES JEANS

Hope is the gay, skylarking pajamas we wear
over yesterday's bruises.
—DE CASSERES

One does not expect in this world; one hopes and
pays carfares.
—JOSEPHINE P. PEABODY

What can be hoped for which is not believed?
—SAINT AUGUSTINE

*H*ope is wanting something so eagerly that—
in spite of all the evidence that you're not
going to get it—you go right on wanting it.
And the remarkable thing about it is that this
very act of hoping produces a kind of strength
of its own.
—NORMAN VINCENT PEALE

*I*f it were not for hopes, the heart would break.
—THOMAS FULLER, M.D.

*P*robably nothing in the world arouses more
false hopes than the first four hours of a diet.
—DAN BENNETT

Hope is putting faith to work when doubting would be easier.

—Anonymous

It is necessary to hope, though hope should always be deluded; for hope itself is happiness, and its frustrations, however frequent, are yet less dreadful than its extinction.

—Samuel Johnson

Hope warps judgment in council, but quickens energy in action.

—Edward Bulwer-Lytton

Know then, whatever cheerful and serene
Supports the mind, supports the body too;
Hence, the most vital movement mortals feel
Is hope, the balm and lifeblood of the soul.
—JOHN ARMSTRONG

Hope is slowly extinguished and quickly
revived.
—SOPHIA LEE

Take hope from the heart of man and you make
him a beast of prey.
—OUIDA

*A*ll this drudgery will kill me if once in a while
   I cannot hope something, for somebody! If I
   cannot sometimes see a bird fly and wave my
   hand to it.
                    —WILLA CATHER

*I*f you do not hope, you will not find what is
   beyond your hopes.
                    —SAINT CLEMENT OF ALEXANDRIA

*W*hat one hopes for is always better than what
   one has.
                    —ETHIOPIAN PROVERB

*H*ope can be neither affirmed nor denied. Hope
is like a path in the countryside: originally
there was no path—yet, as people are walking
all the time in the same spot, a way appears.
——Lu Xun

*H*old your head high, stick your chest out.
You can make it. It gets dark sometimes but
morning comes. . . . Keep hope alive.
——Reverend Jesse Jackson

ingenuity

*N*ever tell people how to do things. Tell them what to do and they will surprise you with their ingenuity.

—George S. Patton

*T*here is one thing stronger than all the armies in the world, and that is an idea whose time has come.

—Victor Hugo

*S*ignificant inventions are not mere accidents. . . .
Happenstance usually plays a part, to be sure,
but there is much more to invention than the
popular notion of a bolt out of the blue.
Knowledge in depth and in breadth are virtual
prerequisites. Unless the mind is thoroughly
changed beforehand, the proverbial spark of
genius, if it should manifest itself, probably will
find nothing to ignite.
——PAUL FLORY

*T*he fellow who invented the Life-Saver really
made a mint.
——GORDON YARDY

Good ideas need landing gear as well as wings.
—C. D. JACKSON

I just invent, then wait until man comes around to needing what I've invented.
—R. BUCKMINSTER FULLER

In trying to make something new, half the undertaking lies in discovering whether it can be done. Once it has been established that it can, duplication is inevitable.
—HELEN GAHAGEN DOUGLAS

There is nothing mysterious about originality,
nothing fantastic. Originality is merely the
step beyond.
—Louis Danz

From every scrap you make a blanket.
—Rose Chernin

One of the greatest pains to human nature is the
pain of a new idea.
—Walter Bagehot

inspiration

A god has his abode within our breast; when he
rouses us, the glow of inspiration warms us;
this holy rapture springs from the seeds of the
divine mind sown in man.
— OVID

*A*s I grow older, part of my emotional survival
plan must be to actively seek inspiration
instead of passively waiting for it to find me.
— BEBE MOORE CAMPBELL

There is something in our minds like sunshine and
the weather, which is not under our control.
When I write, the best things come to me from
I know not where.
— G. C. LICTENBERG

Listen to the voices.
— WILLIAM FAULKNER

A spur in the head is worth two in the heel.
— PROVERB

*Y*ou can't wait for inspiration. You have to go
after it with a club.
—JACK LONDON

*A*ll you have to do is close your eyes and wait for
the symbols.
—IGOR STRAVINSKY

*I*nspiration is the act of drawing up a chair to the
writing desk.
—ANONYMOUS

*A*s long as you're going to think anyway, think
  big.
  —DONALD TRUMP

I dare not alter these things; they come to me
  from above.
  —ALFRED AUSTIN

*I*t usually happens that the more faithfully a person follows the inspirations he receives, the
  more does he experience new inspirations
  which ask increasingly more of him.
  —JOSEPH DE GUIBERT

*D*o not quench your inspiration and your imagination; do not become the slave of your model.
——VINCENT VAN GOGH

I did not write it. God wrote it. I merely did his
dictation.
——HARRIET BEECHER STOWE

*W*hat do you do when inspiration doesn't come:
be careful not to spook, get the wind up, or
force things into position. You must wait
around until the idea comes.
——JOHN HUSTON

To see a world in a grain of sand
And a heaven in a wild flower,
Hold infinity in the palm of your hand
And eternity in an hour.
　　　　　—WILLIAM BLAKE

Ninety percent of inspiration is perspiration.
　　　　　—PROVERB

We cannot carry on inspiration and make it con-
secutive. One day there is no electricity in the
air, and the next the world bristles with sparks
like a cat's back.
　　　　　—RALPH WALDO EMERSON

optimism

I want to see how life can triumph.

—ROMARE BEARDEN

*T*he essence of optimism is that it takes no account
of the present, but it is a source of inspiration,
of vitality and hope where others have
resigned; it enables a man to hold his head
high, to claim the future for himself and not
to abandon it to his enemy.

—DIETRICH BONHOEFFER

*A*h, but a man's reach should exceed his grasp—
or what's a heaven for?

———Robert Browning

I am satisfied with, and stand firm as a rock on,
the belief that all that happens in God's world
is for the best, but what is merely germ, what
blossom, and what fruit I do not know.

———J. G. Fichte

[*O*ptimism is] making the most of all that comes
and the least of all that goes.

———Anonymous

*W*hat seems to be a great loss or punishment often turns out to be a blessing. I know, through my own experience, that God never closes one door without opening another.

—Yolande D. Herron

*T*he optimist proclaims that we live in the best of all possible worlds; and the pessimist fears this is true.

—James Branch Cabell

*A*n optimist is a man who starts a crossword puzzle with a fountain pen.

—Anonymous

A pessimist is someone who complains about the noise when opportunity knocks.
— MICHAEL LEVINE

*W*e cheerfully assume that in some mystic way love conquers all, that good outweighs evil in the just balances of the universe and that at the eleventh hour something gloriously triumphant will prevent the worst before it happens.
— BROOKS ATKINSON

*I*t is worth a thousand pounds a year to have the habit of looking on the bright side of things.
— SAMUEL JOHNSON

The outstanding characteristic of America is the refusal of Americans to accept defects in their society as irremediable.

—LEWIS GALANTIERE

It's simpler to be an optimist and it's a sensible defense against the uncertainties and abysses which otherwise confront us prematurely—we can die a dozen deaths and then usually we find that the outcome is not one we predicted, neither so "bad" nor so "good," but one we hadn't taken into consideration.

—EDWARD HOAGLAND

I hold not with the pessimist that all things are ill,
nor with the optimist that all things are well.
All things are not well, but all things shall be
well, because this is God's world.
— ROBERT BROWNING

An optimist is a driver who thinks that
empty space at the curb won't have a hydrant
beside it.
— *CHANGING TIMES*

Pessimism wilts everything around it.
— MICHAEL LEVINE

An optimist may see a light where there is none,
but why must the pessimist always run to blow
it out?
— MICHEL DE SAINT-PIERRE

Twixt optimist and pessimist
The difference is droll:
The optimist sees the doughnut,
The pessimist, the hole.
— MCLANDBURGH WILSON

For myself I am an optimist—it does not seem
to be much use being anything else.
— WINSTON CHURCHILL

*L*et other pens dwell on guilt and misery.
— JANE AUSTEN

*I*f I didn't have spiritual faith, I would be a
pessimist. But I'm an optimist. I've read the
last page in the Bible. It's all going to turn
out all right.
— BILLY GRAHAM

*I*t's such an act of optimism to get through a day
and enjoy it and laugh and do all that without
thinking about death. What spirit human
beings have!
— GILDA RADNER

*G*ray skies are just clouds passing over.
——DUKE ELLINGTON

*W*e are all in the gutter, but some of us are
looking at the stars.
——OSCAR WILDE

*I*t will all come right in the wash.
——PROVERB

*T*wo men look out through the same bars:
One sees the mud, and one the stars.
——FREDERICK LANGBRIDGE

If you think you'll lose, you're lost,
For out in the world we find
Success begins with a fellow's will;
It's all in the state of mind.
Life's battles don't always go
To the stronger or faster man;
But soon or late the man who wins
Is the man who thinks he can.

—WALTER D. WINTLE

Become a possibilitarian. No matter how dark
things seem to be or actually are, raise your
sights and see the possibilities—always see
them, for they're always there.

—NORMAN VINCENT PEALE

Optimism doesn't wait on facts. It deals with prospects. Pessimism is a waste of time.

—Norman Cousins

The greatest discovery of my generation is that a human being can alter his life by altering his attitudes of mind.

—William James

When pessimists think they're taking a chance, optimists feel they're grasping a great opportunity.

—Anonymous

The year's at the spring
And day's at the morn;
Morning's at seven;
The hillside's dew-pearled;
The lark's on the wing;
The snail's on the thorn:
God's in his heaven—
All's right with the world!

—ROBERT BROWNING

The American, by nature, is optimistic. He is
experimental, an inventor, and a builder who
builds best when called upon to build greatly.

—JOHN F. KENNEDY

All my life I've had this almost criminal
optimism. I didn't care what happened,
the glass was always going to be half full.
—QUINCY JONES

This the best day the world has ever seen.
Tomorrow will be better.
—R. A. CAMPBELL

Like the Mississippi, it just keeps rolling along.
Let it roll. Let it roll on full flood, inexorable,
irresistible, benignant, to broader lands and
better days.
—WINSTON CHURCHILL

An optimist is the human personification of spring.
— SUSAN J. BISSONETTE

When you have only two pennies left in the world, buy a loaf of bread with one, and a lily with the other.
— CHINESE PROVERB

Write it in your heart that every day is the best day in the year.
— RALPH WALDO EMERSON

*S*hoot for the moon. Even if you miss it you will
land among the stars.
— LES BROWN

*P*ositive thinking is the key to success in
business, education, pro football, anything
that you can mention. I go out there thinking
that I am going to complete every pass.
— RON JAWORSKI

*S*in is behovely, but all shall be well and all shall
be well and all manner of thing shall be well.
— JULIAN OF NORWICH

piety

The strength of a man consists in finding out the
way in which God is going, and going in that
way too.
—HENRY WARD BEECHER

The great religious texts throughout the ages
wouldn't always be exhorting us to do good if
they didn't recognize that we're inclined, so
often, to do evil.
—MICHAEL LEVINE

*S*et your affections on things above, not on things
on the earth.

——Colossians 3:2

*I*t is rash to intrude upon the piety of others: both
the depth and the grace of it elude the stranger.

——George Santayana

*P*iety is not an end, but a means: a means of
attaining the highest culture through the purest
tranquility of soul.

——Johann Wolfgang von Goethe

The best way to see divine light is to put out thy own candle.

—THOMAS FULLER, M.D.

Piety requires us to renounce no ways of life where we can act reasonably, and offer what we do to the glory of God.

—WILLIAM LAW

Live with men as if God saw you: speak to God as if men heard you.

—SENECA

faith

*T*his I do believe above all, especially in my times of greater discouragement, that I must believe—that I must believe in my fellow men—that I must believe in myself—and I must believe in God—if life is to have any meaning.

—MARGARET CHASE SMITH

*F*aith is the choice of the nobler alternative.

—DEAN WILLIAM R. INGE

As he that fears God fears nothing else, so, he that sees God sees everything else.
—JOHN DONNE

I share Einstein's affirmation that anyone who is not lost on the rapturous awe at the power and glory of the mind behind the universe "is as good as a burnt out candle."
—MADELEINE L'ENGLE

Faith is not a formula which is agreed to if the weight of evidence favors it.
—WALTER LIPPMANN

*V*igorous questioning can propel a restoration and
   deepening of conviction. Skepticism is a phase,
   not an internal condition; out of the embryo of
   uncertainty grows the examination that produces a deeper, common, more genuine conviction. Paradoxically, it is the very questioning
   that causes the rubbing that polishes the pearl.
   —MICHAEL LEVINE

*I*t is your own assent to yourself, and the constant
   voice of your own reason, and not of others,
   that should make you believe.
   —BLAISE PASCAL

For as the body without the spirit is dead, so faith without works is dead also.

— JAMES 2:26

Faith is, before all and above all, wishing God may exist.

— MIGUEL DE UNAMUNO

Faith is a knowledge of the benevolence of God toward us, and a certain persuasion of His veracity.

— JOHN CALVIN

*F*aith is the antiseptic of the soul.
— WALT WHITMAN

*F*aith is kept alive in us, and gathers strength,
more from practice than from speculations.
— JOSEPH ADDISON

*A*nd I said to the man who stood at the gate of
the year, "Give me a light that I may tread
safely into the unknown." And he replied,
"Go out into the darkness and put your hand
into the hand of God. That shall be to you
better than light and safer than a known way."
— LOUISE HASKINS

*I*t is consciousness itself . . . which can suggest that
there is God. For it is the hint that there can
exist something very real that is more than the
merely physical.
—BARRY HOLTZ

*Y*es, I have doubted. I have wandered off the
path. I have been lost. But I always returned. It
is beyond the logic I seek. It is intuitive—an
intrinsic, built-in sense of direction. I seem to
find my way home. My faith has wavered but
has saved me.
—HELEN HAYES

The most satisfying and ecstatic faith is almost
    purely agnostic. It trusts absolutely without
professing to know at all.
                        —H. L. MENCKEN

We are not human beings trying to be spiritual.
    We are spiritual beings trying to be human.
                        —JACQUELYN SMALL

Faith is much better than belief. Belief is when
    someone *else* does the thinking.
                        —R. BUCKMINSTER FULLER

*Y*ou can't solve many of today's problems by straight linear thinking. It takes leaps of faith to sense the connections that are not necessarily obvious.

—MATINA HORNER

I would not attack the faith of a heathen without being sure I had a better one to put in its place.

—HARRIET BEECHER STOWE

*I*f there was no faith there would be no living in this world. We couldn't even eat hash with any safety.

—JOSH BILLINGS

There lives more faith in honest doubt,
Believe me, than in half the creeds.
—ALFRED, LORD TENNYSON

Console thyself, thou wouldst not seek Me, if thou
hadst not found Me.
—BLAISE PASCAL

Faith embraces itself and the doubt about itself.
—PAUL TILLICH

Faith is never identical with piety.
—KARL BARTH

The world has a thousand creeds, and never a one
    have I;
Nor a church of my own, though a thousand spires
    are pointing way on high.
But I float on the bosom of faith, that bears me
    along like a river;
And the lamp of my soul is alight with love for life,
    and the world, and the Giver.
            —ELLA WHEELER WILCOX

A man consists of the faith that is in him.
    Whatever his faith is, he is.
            —BHAGAVAD GITA

*F*aith is not a series of gilt-edged propositions
that you sit down to figure out, and if you
follow all the logic and accept all the
conclusions, then you have it. It is crumpling
and throwing away everything, proposition
by proposition, until nothing is left, and then
writing a new proposition, your very own, to
throw in the teeth of despair.
—MARY JEAN IRION

*T*hink of only three things—your God, your
family, and the Green Bay Packers—in
that order.
—VINCE LOMBARDI

*T*oday you can post the Ten Commandments in
Moscow public schools, but it is illegal to do
it in the United States.
———MICHAEL LEVINE

I respect faith, but doubt is what gets you an
education.
———WILSON MIZNER

*T*he great act of faith is when man decides that
he is not God.
———OLIVER WENDELL HOLMES JR.

*W*e live by faith or we do not live at all. Either
we venture—or we vegetate. If we venture,
we do so by faith simply because we cannot
know the end of anything at its beginning.
We risk marriage on faith or we stay single.
We prepare for a profession by faith or we
give up before we start. By faith we move
mountains of opposition or we are stopped
by molehills.

—HAROLD WALKER

A person can do other things against his will;
but belief is possible only in one who is willing.

—SAINT AUGUSTINE

If you have any faith, give me, for heaven's sake, a share of it! Your doubts you may keep to yourself, I have plenty of my own.

—JOHANN WOLFGANG VON GOETHE

My reason nourishes my faith and my faith my reason.

—NORMAN COUSINS

To believe only possibilities is not faith, but mere philosophy.

—SIR THOMAS BROWNE

*L*et us have faith that right makes might; and in that faith let us dare to do our duty as we understand it.

—ABRAHAM LINCOLN

I do not feel obliged to believe that the same God who has endowed us with sense, reason, and intellect, has intended us to forgo their use.

—GALILEO

*F*aith, like a jackal, feeds among the tombs, and even from these dead doubts she gathers her most vital hope.

—HERMAN MELVILLE

Conversion for me was not a Damascus Road experience. I slowly moved into an intellectual acceptance of what my intuition had always known.

—MADELEINE L'ENGLE

Faith is to believe what you do not yet see; the reward for this faith is to see what you believe.

—SAINT AUGUSTINE

I would rather live in a world where my life is surrounded by mystery than live in a world so small that my mind could comprehend it.

—HARRY EMERSON FOSDICK

Skepticism is the beginning of faith.

—GEORGE BERNARD SHAW

Treat the other man's faith gently; it is all he has to believe with.

—HENRY S. HASKINS

If you can't have faith in what is held up to you for faith, you must find things to believe in yourself, for a life without faith in something is too narrow a space to live.

—GEORGE E. WOODBURY

*W*e must have infinite faith in each other. If we have not, we must never let it leak out that we have not.
——HENRY DAVID THOREAU

*F*aith is not *being sure.* It is *not being sure,* but betting with your last cent.
——MARY JEAN IRION

*W*e have not lost faith, but we have transferred it from God to the medical profession.
——GEORGE BERNARD SHAW

A faith that cannot survive collision with the
truth is not worth many regrets.
——Arthur C. Clarke

*T*he twenty-first century will be religious or will
not be at all.
——André Malraux

*Q*uestion with boldness even the existence of
God; because, if there be one, he must more
approve of the homage of reason than that of
blindfolded fear.
——Thomas Jefferson

*T*here is one thing higher than Royalty: and that is religion, which causes us to leave the world, and seek God.

— ELIZABETH I

*P*eople see God every day. They just don't recognize him.

— PEARL BAILEY

'*T*want me, 'twas the Lord. I always told Him, "I trust you. I don't know where to go or what to do, but I expect you to lead me." And He always did.

— HARRIET TUBMAN

*R*eal faith is not the stuff dreams are made of; rather it is tough, practical and altogether realistic. Faith sees the invisible but it does not see the nonexistent.

—A. W. TOZER

*F*aith affirms what the senses do not affirm, but not the contrary of what they perceive. It is above, and not contrary to.

—BLAISE PASCAL

*F*aith is the belief of the heart in that knowledge which comes from the Unseen.

—MUHAMMAD BEN KAFIF

*F*aith is not making religious-sounding noises in the daytime. It is asking your inmost self questions at night—and then getting up and going to work.
—MARY JEAN IRION

*F*aith is raising the sail of our little boat until it is caught up in the soft winds above and picks up speed. . . .
—RALPH W. WARD

*F*aith is the force of life.
—LEO TOLSTOY

*F*aith is a kind of winged intellect. The great workmen of history have been men who believed like giants.

——CHARLES HENRY PARK

*T*he principal part of faith is patience.

——GEORGE MACDONALD

*M*an's creed is that he believes in God, and therefore in mankind, but not that he believes in creed.

——LEO BAECK

As the flower is before the fruit, so is faith before good works.

—RICHARD WHATELY

I am full-fed and yet I hunger. What means this deep hunger in my heart?

—ALFRED NOYES

We have only to believe, then little by little we shall see the universal horror unbend and then smile upon us.

—PIERRE TEILHARD DE CHARDIN

*A*ll the scholastic scaffolding falls, as a ruined
edifice, before one single word—faith.
—NAPOLEON I

*U*nless there is within us that which is above us,
we shall soon yield to that which is about us.
—PETER TAYLOR FORSYTH

*I*t is cynicism and fear that freeze life; it is faith
that thaws it out, releases it, sets it free.
—HARRY EMERSON FOSDICK

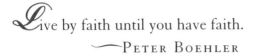

*L*ive by faith until you have faith.
—PETER BOEHLER

*O*rthodoxy can be learned from others; living faith must be a matter of personal experience.
—J. W. BUCHSEL

*F*aith is the daring of the soul to go farther than it can see.
—WILLIAM NEWTON CLARKE

I believe in the incomprehensibility of God.
—HONORÉ DE BALZAC

*D*oubt is not the opposite of faith; it is one
element of faith.
— PAUL TILLICH

*F*aith is the substance of things hoped for,
the evidence of things not seen.
— HEBREWS 11:1

*T*he care of God for us is a great thing,
if a man believe it at heart:
it plucks the burden of sorrow from him.
— EURIPIDES

*I*f you have abandoned one faith, do not abandon all faith. There is always an alternative to the faith we lose. Or is it the same faith under another mask?
— GRAHAM GREENE

*F*aith is a living and unshakeable confidence, a belief in the grace of God so assured that a man would die a thousand deaths for its sake.
— MARTIN LUTHER

*F*aith is the state of being ultimately concerned.
— PAUL TILLICH

*B*elieve that you have it, and you have it.
———Desiderius Erasmus

*F*aith builds a bridge across the gulf of death.
———Edward Young

*N*o man has power to let another prescribe his faith. Faith is not faith without believing.
———Thomas Jefferson

*N*ot Truth, but Faith it is that keeps the world alive.
———Edna St. Vincent Millay

I pray hard, work hard, and leave the rest to God.
　　　　　—FLORENCE GRIFFITH JOYNER

We cannot live on probabilities. The faith in
which we can live bravely and die in peace
must be a certainty, so far as it professes to
be a faith at all, or it is nothing.
　　　　　—J. A. FROUDE

There is no unbelief;
Whoever plants a seed beneath the sod
And waits to see it push away the clod,
He trusts in God.
　　　　　—ELIZABETH YORK CASE

The only known cure for fear is faith.
—LENA KELLOGG SADLER

Let nothing disturb you. Let nothing frighten
you. Everything passes away except God.
—SAINT THERESA OF JESUS

Faith is an excitement and an enthusiasm; it is
a condition of intellectual magnificence to
which we must cling as to a treasure and not
squander in . . . priggish argument.
—GEORGE SAND

*I*f it can be verified, we don't need faith. . . .
Faith is for that which lies on the *other* side of
reason. Faith is what makes life bearable, with
all its tragedies and ambiguities and sudden,
startling joys.

———Madeleine L'Engle

*I*t seems to me that in our time faith in God is the
same thing as faith in good and the ultimate
triumph of good over evil.

———Svetlana Alliluyeva

I could prove God statistically.

———George Gallup

I had rather believe all the fables in the Legend and the Talmud and the Alcoran than that this universal frame is without a mind.
—FRANCIS BACON

F aith is not a momentary feeling, but a struggle against the discouragement that threatens us every time we meet with resistance.
—BAKOLE WA ILUNGA

W hen one has faith, then he thinks. One who lacks faith does not think.
—CHANDOGYA UPANISHAD

I never talked with God,
Nor visited in Heaven—
Yet certain am I of the spot
As if the chart were given.

—EMILY DICKINSON

He will not enter hell who hath faith equal to
a single grain of mustard seed in his heart.

—MUHAMMAD

Blessed are they that have not seen, and yet
have believed.

—JOHN 20:29

*I*f you believe, then you hang on. If you believe, it means you've got imagination, you don't need stuff thrown out for you in a blueprint.

—RUTH GORDON

*F*aith, in its very nature, demands action. Faith is action—never a passive attitude.

—PAUL E. LITTLE

*Y*ou can keep a faith only as you can keep a plant, by rooting it into your life and making it grow.

—PHILLIPS BROOKS

*F*aith faces everything that makes the world
uncomfortable—pain, fear, loneliness, shame,
death—and acts with a compassion by which
these things are transformed, even exalted.
—SAMUEL H. MILLER

*F*aith is like the little night-light that burns in a
sickroom; as long as it is there, the obscurity is
not complete, we turn toward it and await the
daylight.
—ABBE HUVELIN

THE TEXT OF THIS BOOK IS SET IN GRANJON
BY MSPACE, KATONAH, NEW YORK.

BOOK DESIGN BY MAURA FADDEN ROSENTHAL